From Bard To Verse

An anthology of humorous poetry

Steven Pearlman

ISBN: 978-1-4834-1914-5 (sc)
ISBN: 978-1-4834-1326-6 (e)

Because of the dynamic nature of the Internet, any web addresses or
links contained in this book may have changed since publication and may
no longer be valid. The views expressed in this work are solely those
of the author and do not necessarily reflect the views of the publisher,
and the publisher hereby disclaims any responsibility for them.

Any people depicted in stock imagery provided by Thinkstock are
models, and such images are being used for illustrative purposes only.
Certain stock imagery © Thinkstock.

Lulu Publishing Services rev. date: 9/30/2014

Contents

Albert Einstein and My Mum

Okay, Albert Einstein was clever,

As brilliant as they come,

But when it comes to time, space and energy,

There's none could compete with my mum.

She always had time for her children,

Gave us space when we needed it too,

And she worked and she cleaned and she cooked

With the energy of chimps in a zoo.

She was filled with homely wisdom,

Gleaned more from life than school,

And as for relativity,

This relative was nobody's fool.

We even lived on Albert Avenue;

It's true – I tell you no lies,

And is it just mere coincidence

That her maiden name was Allweis?*

So you see there's quite an affinity

Between Einstein and my mum,

But she swapped 'e equals mc squared'

For a simpler 'e by gum'.

(* Pronounced 'allwise')

An Alphabet of Unpleasantness

A is for apples with creatures inside.

B is boyfriends, or girlfriends, who lied.

C is for chewing gum stuck on your shoe.

D is for desperate but where's the loo?

E is for eggs you drop on the floor.

F is for football and you can't score.

G is for guests who aren't any fun.

H is for holiday without the sun.

I is for indigestion pain.

J is for jackpot? Lost again!

K is for keys that simply aren't there.

L is for lice that crawl in your hair.

M is for meals you can't afford.

N is for nails scraping a board.

O is for onions on someone's breath.

P is for partner who nags you to death.

Q is for quarrels with brothers and sisters.

R is for running so much, you get blisters.

S is for smell of unwashed feet.

T is for treading on poo in the street.

U is for ugly facial blotching.

V is for videos you were caught watching!

W for waiting, too long, on your own.

X is for X-ray – you've broken a bone!

Y is for yogurt that feels like slime.

Z for zero out of ten for this rhyme!

The Animal Shrink

I am a veterinary psychiatrist;
That's animal shrink to you.
Bring me your pet,
If it's feeling upset,
And I'll see what I can do.
If your budgie refuses to budge,
If your rooster simply won't roost,
Or your dog will not walk,
Or your parrot won't talk,
Then I'll try to give them a boost.
If your horse has a very long face,
If your crocodile's too snappy,
Or your little pup
Is really fed up,
I'll try to make them feel happy.
If your buffalo's feeling baffled,
If your deer has no idea,
Or if your kangaroos
Are a little confused,
I'll try to make everything clear.
If your insects are going insane,
If your jellyfish simply won't gel,
Or if your iguanas
Are completely bananas,
I'll help them 'cos I'm mad as well!

A Brief History of the World

Scientists say the world began
Five billion years ago.
It might have been a Tuesday,
But I don't really know.
At first the Earth was really hot,
But then began to cool,
And from within a bubbling swamp,
Appeared a special molecule.
This was the earliest form of life -
A simple, single cell.
It wasn't terribly advanced,
And couldn't read or write too well.
More life-forms developed,
Like basic fish and plants.
Creatures crawled out of the water,
Looking shy without any pants!
Then creepy-crawlies emerged,
The irritating things,
And just to make it worse,
Some developed wings!
Then along came the dinosaur;
He was so big and daft,
That if something tickled his tail,
It was a minute before he laughed!
Then the birds evolved,
To dominate the skies,

And sometimes drop their business
Into other creatures' eyes!
Then along came the mammals:
The shrew, the rabbit, the pig,
(The dinosaurs had long died out,
'Cos they were far too big!)
Next the monkeys, oo-oo!
Some learnt to walk upright.
This was the start of mankind,
If you think Darwin was right!
Early man went hunting,
And began to use some tools.
He could make fire from flintstones,
(Not Fred and Barney, you fools!)
Religions and language developed,
And the first attempts at writing.
A few were inventing the wheel,
But the main pastime was fighting!
Then people began to farm:
Towns and villages grew.
Clever societies flourished,
And a couple of thick ones too!
The Sumerians were good with numbers,
The Egyptians left pyramids as proof,
The Druids built Stonehenge,
But they still haven't added a roof!
The Chinese made many inventions
And a wall that none could pass,

The Mycenaeans had treasure a-plenty
And the Phoenicians were smashing with glass!
The Babylonians were good at building,
The Greeks were good at maths,
The Romans used to make straight roads
And lounge around in baths.
Then came the conquering Vikings,
The gallant knight on stallion,
Then ships explored the Americas,
Doing fifty miles to the galleon!
Meanwhile Caxton and Gutenberg
Gave us the printed letter,
And someone invented the gun,
So we could kill much better!
Art and literature thrived,
Empires would rise and fall,
Electric machines were invented,
Which came as a shock to us all!
Then came cars and aeroplanes,
Two World Wars, TV,
The Space Age and computers -
Now this poem is history!

Bags of Versatility

Let's hear it for the plastic bag;
To me, an unsung hero.
It has so many uses
And its cost is often zero.
You can use it for shopping,
Or for a muddy ball.
They're useful on a holiday
If your suitcase is too small.
Use one for your litter
If there is no bin about.
Use one to cure your hiccups -
Just breathe in and out!
A tramp can use a bag
To carry all his things.
A swimmer can use two of them
As makeshift water-wings!
Use one as a cover
To protect a tasty dish;
Use one at the fairground
To carry home your fish!
Use one when it's raining
As a temporary hat;
Use one to dispose of
The messes from your cat.
There is just one more use,
As yet I haven't said:
Put a bag, with holes in,
Over your ugly head!

Building a Better Future?

(Written 27-8-03. I, a teacher at the time, was about to return to
work after the summer holidays...)
I popped into the Junior School
Not expecting trouble,
But the scene that met my eyes
Was one of mess and rubble.
I was hoping all these workmen
Might have worked a little faster,
But the hall was like a warehouse,
My classroom a total disaster.
The place was simply swarming
With builders and electricians,
But if we're to be ready by Monday,
We need to employ magicians.
The head looked rather shell-shocked,
The caretaker bemused.
The parents were very concerned,
But the kids were most amused!
The campus resembled a bomb-site,
As the place was developed, rewired.
I'm normally quite compassionate,
But these 'workers' should be fired!
But every cloud (of plaster and dust)
Does have a silver lining,
So if I get a longer holiday,
Perhaps I should stop whining!

Buy, Buy, Lion King!

Dan once saw 'The Lion King'
And thought it was so great,
He got his dad to buy him
A Lion King cup and plate.
Then a Lion King t-shirt
And of course the video;
Next, some Lion King pyjamas -
His dad just couldn't say no.
Then some Lion King stationery
And a Lion King pencil case,
Followed by a Lion King toothbrush
And a watch with a Lion King face.
One day Dan's dad was furious -
He saw the Lion King stuff in the bin.
"The Lion King's out of date!" said Dan,
"But Pocohontas is in!
I want the Pocohontas t-shirt
And the Pocohontas game,
And Ben's got a Pocohontas duvet;
Please can I have the same?"
"Well," said Dan's dad calmly,
"I've just seen 'The Invisible Man',
So here's an invisible hundred pounds -
Go and buy whatever you can!

Chalk and Cheese

We're not compatible, you and I,
Yet we are together; I don't know why.
I like noise but you like quiet.
I like to eat but you like to diet.
I like to jog but you like to walk.
I like telly but you like to talk.
I like Blackpool, you like France.
I'm a bit clumsy but you can dance.
I like rock music, you like folk.
I'm into ghosts; you think they're a joke.
What I think's funny, you think's daft.
What I call fresh air, you call draught.
You like lettuce, I like meat.
You play properly, I like to cheat.
You like kittens, I like gorillas.
You like rom coms, I like thrillers.
You like mange tout, I like beans.
You dress smartly, I like jeans.
You are cautious, I am rash.
You drive carefully, I tend to crash.
You like tennis, I like soccer.
You are sane, I'm off my rocker.
We're not compatible, you and I,
But we're still together; I don't know why.

Chocs Away!

(This poem was written in response to the Headmaster's habit of giving his staff numerous boxes of chocolates at the end of every term.)

Of course we thank our leader, Peter;
As gestures go, there's nothing sweeter,
But therein lies the trouble, you see,
As dentists rub their hands with glee.
I fill my face with fat and sugar,
'Cos I'm a weak and greedy......person!
Now some might say, "Oh Pearlman, quiet!"
But think of every woman's diet!
What happens to their thin agenda
When they go on a chocolate bender?
"So what do you suggest?" they say.
Well I propose a healthier way;
Broccoli, spinach, corn on the cob
Are healthier fare to fill your gob.
Carrot batons and celery sticks
Should replace the Mars and Twix.
Bananas, apples and strawberries
Are preferable to Cadbury's.
And so I make this plea today:
Please Mr Parker – chocs away!

Clever Clive

When Clever Clive was only two,
He had a really high IQ.
He'd learnt the rudiments of chess
And could tackle crosswords, more or less.
When Clever Clive had turned just three,
He spoke at functions for a fee.
He taught himself to dance ballet
And built a rather nice chalet.
When Clever Clive was only four,
He helped his dad at corporate law.
He could speak and read Chinese,
He found a cure for heart disease.
But then this genius turned five;
It proved a difficult time for Clive.
He had to start attending school,
Where everyone else seemed such a fool.
Clive didn't really want to go;
There was nothing else to know!
He found it all a dreadful bore -
The teachers asked HIM when they weren't sure!
The children thought him rather strange.
Clive decided – things must change.
So he whacked his head with a household brick
And now he's happy being slightly thick!

Crimary School

I know a school for criminals,
The headmaster's called Nick.
The baddies are the scholars,
And the honest ones are thick.
On Monday they learn bribery
And techniques of "persuasion".
Then a politician comes
And teaches tax evasion.
On Tuesday it's deception,
So you know how to con,
And how to pinch men's wallets
So they don't know that they're gone.
Wednesday mornings – kidnapping,
(A new subject this year)
But strangely, in the afternoon,
Some children disappear.
On Thursday most learn violence;
They find it rather thrilling,
And the more advanced exponents
Take a special course in killing.
On Friday it is arson,
Where kids play fiery games.
We know when they're successful -
The school's engulfed in flames!

A Cup of Bitter

(Written by me in bitter Manchester United fan mode the day after
Liverpool's remarkable Champions' League win on 26th May, 2006.)

You think you're the best in Europe?
You must be 'avin a larf!
Just because somehow you managed
To score three goals in one half.
Your second goal was clearly offside,
The linesman was waving his flag -
Then, a few seconds later,
Smicer found the onion bag.
And AC Milan had a good goal
Ruled out for being offside,
But it came to him from a Scouser,
So why was Shevchenko denied?
And as for that late double-save,
How lucky can one team get?
'Cos 99 times out of a hundred,
The ball would have been in the net.
And Benitez a tactical master?
Now I know you're taking the mick.
He picked Harry Kewell for starters -
You're lucky he cried off sick!
Anyway, you shouldn't have been there;
You know I'm not one to whine,
But that 'goal' you scored against Chelsea -
The ball wasn't over the line!
So the shell-suits, the perms and the tashes
Are filling the streets in their glee.
I suppose you'll be nicking some champagne -
I suppose it's just bitter for me!

Current Affairs

I don't know watt went wrong.
I've no idea wire girl like you
Would switch allegiance so suddenly.
One minute I'm the light of your life,
So bright and sensor-ble apparently,
But then you met Phil Ament,
That fuse-leer from Ampstead.
The atmosphere became highly charged.
You became re-volting.
You came in su late every night.
I was so lenoid with you -
In fact incandescent with rage.
I felt like committing assault and battery
But I know how to conduct myself.
Then fortunately I met Ann Ode.
We both felt a spark instantly.
I just can't resistor.
We're going to set up ohm together
In a static caravan
Somewhere near Leads.
But your behaviour was shocking
And still hertz.

Dial-ogue

(An imaginary conversation with the speaking clock woman)

I heard that your grandfather died
At his second attempt
To climb Ben Nevis.
"At the third"
What did he die of?
"Stroke"
Listen – I believe it's going to be
A lovely evening tonight.
"It will be"
Perhaps we could go for a walk?
"To?"
Anywhere really.
What time do you have
To be in tonight?
"Nine"
What? Does that mean
You don't have the time for me?
"Precisely."

Feeling Horse

We had such a stable relationship.
You were as sweet as Shergar
And I was your mane man.
You even began to look at bridle dresses.
I'd wake up joyfilly every day.
But that didn't last furlong.
Yes I made some foalish mistakes,
And got saddled with debt.
But hay - isn't that just the Epsom Downs of life?
I thought we could overcome that hurdle.
You say Ascot nothing to do with it,
But why did you suddenly become so colt-hearted?
You began to take a fence so easily.
We had that luxury weekend in Canterbury -
A fetlock of good that did.
We argued three days on the trot.
It gave me such a Haydock.
You just Aintreely bothered about making it work.
Then you began to get too friendly with your neigh-bour,
Hoof ell for your undoubted charms.
Now he reins supreme
And I'm having a mare.

Football Freddy

Football Freddy is unique;
He's the original football freak.
Eating, sleeping, breathing soccer -
People think he's off his rocker.
Ninety percent of his conversation
Is about this fascination.
He hardly bothered with school at all;
He much preferred to kick a ball,
Or read a football magazine,
Or study the game on a massive screen.
He gathers football memorabilia
And is a font of football trivia.
He knows the result of every game
And can tell you every scorer's name.
He can even name the referee
And what the goalie had for tea!
He follows his team on every trip,
Wearing the latest costly strip.
From Plymouth up to Aberdeen -
You name the ground and Freddy's been.
He plays up front for a local side
And though his shots fly high and wide,
He still clings on to a precious dream
That he'll one day play for his favourite team.
It's all a bit sad, you must agree,
'Cos Football Freddy is forty three!

Fruit Basket Cases

I am appeeling to you
And would be grapeful for any help.
You see all my fruits are basket cases.
My blueberries are feeling blue,
My passion fruit has lost its passion,
My loquats are feeling low,
And my pears are in despear.
My raisins are currantly on medication
And my currants have lost all raisin to live.
My ugli fruit cannot face it
And my peach has capeachulated.
Some of my melons are meloncholy,
Others have gone cantaloopy.
I have morosehips
And crabby apples.
My cherries just want to get stoned
And my olives are to be pitted.
My damsons have plummed the depths
And my banana has a split personality.
I even saw one mango insane.
It's quite exstrawberry.
How can I figs this problem?
Gourd only knows.

Fun-eral

Went to a funeral yesterday -
It actually wasn't too bad.
In fact I had a bit of a giggle
Though I think it was meant to be sad.
The deceased were Siamese twins,
So the coffin was shaped like a Y.
But the hole was only rectangular -
"A grave mistake," said I.
Then one twin woke from a coma;
We gasped as up popped his head.
He said, "Hold on a minute...
There's only one of us dead!"
This was quite a moral dilemma -
It was very confusing to me;
Do you simply bury the dead one,
With the other sticking up like a tree?
On reflection, this poem is weird,
The direction it's taken aint fun.
Let's say he's now a Siametree
And end with that dreadful pun.

Getting Up To Nothing

I could paint the whole town red,
Or perhaps fly off to the Med.
I could even build a garden shed,
If I could only get out of bed.

I could roast a joint of meat,
Pick up litter from the street.
I could even buy a three-piece suite,
If I could just get onto my feet.

I could compose a wonderful tune,
Or go up in a hot air balloon.
I could sell my antique spoon,
If I could get up fairly soon.

I could learn how to milk a cow.
I could hang a swing from a bough.
I could pay a brief visit to Slough,
If I could just get vertical now.

I could clear up last night's mess.
I could grow some mustard and cress.
I could do anything, more or less,
If I could only manage to dress.

But my clothes remain in a heap.
I suppose my ambitions will keep.
It's enough to make you weep,
But I think I'll go back to sleep!

Hello, Goodbye

"Hi!" said the mountaineer.

"Hiya!" said the auctioneer.

"Hire!" said the car rental guy.

"Hullo!" said the man from Humberside.

"Mourning," said the bereaved woman.

"All right?" said the maths teacher.

"How's it going?" said the mechanic.

"Long time no see!" said the mole.

"What's up?" said the helium balloon seller.

"How's it hanging?" said the curtain seller.

"Ciao!" said the Chinese dog.

"Bye!" said the wicket-keeper.

"Have an ice day!" said the polar bear.

"Speak later!" wrote the hopeful mute.

"C u!" said the copper.

"Take air!" said the diver.

"Until we meat again!" said the carnivore.

"So long!" said the snake.

"Catch you later!" said the angler.

"Alf Wiedersehen!" said Alf's friend.

"Must dash!" said Zapata.

"Zionara!" said the Japanese Israeli.

Hero Zeroes

Who can save us now?
Batman just hangs around.
Spiderman's website is down.
The Iron Man's gone rusty.
Aquaman has turned into a drip.
Catwoman isn't feline very well.
Captain America is too Pacific.
Captain Atom has become negative.
The Hulk is now merely credible.
The Green Arrow has become pointless.
Quicksilver has become Slowbronze.
Hercules has become Hercu-less.
The X-Men have all got X-Ma.
The Ninja Turtles are shell-shocked.
Popeye has developed a spinach allergy.
Lancelot has lostalot.
Robin Hood is now a hoodlum.
Sherlock doesn't know Wats on.
Nancy withDrew.
Frodo is ti-ring.
James Bond is now 0.07.
Harry just Potters around.
Hans Solo is now so low.
Even Superman has reached his Lois point.
It's a Marvel we're still here.

Historics

When Archimedes sat in his tub,
Having a wash and quite a good scrub,
He looked down and with mirth did ripple;
He'd discovered his famous principle!
He ran down the street, completely nude.
Everyone stared and said, "How rude!"
He shouted and screamed, "I've done it! Eureka!"
That makes Archimedes the very first streaker!

The Romans invaded a long time ago,
But why leave Italy? I don't know!
They came here in open-toed sandals,
So warmed their feet on Roman candles.
They built straight roads, nice baths, a good wall,
So for invaders, they weren't bad at all!
After four hundred years, they had to go home.
After all that roamin', they went back to Rome!

When Sir Walter Raleigh went looking for goods,
He returned to Queen Liz with tobacco and spuds.
She lit up and coughed, "You've got to be joking!"
He replied, "Well that's a potato you're smoking!
I must have confused you. Sorry – my fault.
You boil potatoes and mash them with salt."
Liz ordered some mash, licking her lips,
But after she'd tried it, said, "Please invent chips!"

Holiday Advice

Shipbuilders should go to Hull!
Go to Dulwich if you're dull.
Sailors, why not go to Crewe?
Diarrhoea? Visit Looe!
Apiarists, try St Bees!
Or Sevenoaks if you like trees!
Cricket ball-makers – go to Cork!
Try Chatsworth if you like to talk!
To Whitby if you are a joker,
Or Card-iff you're keen on poker!
Maybe Rugby – worth a try?
Philosophers should go to Wye.
If you're balding, visit Ayr,
Stallions - try Weston-super-Mare!
If you like dirt, go to Muck,
Or go to Reading for a book.
In some trouble? Go to Hyde.
If you're bonny, go to Clyde!
Try Bedford if you're feeling tired,
Or Bury if you've just expired!

In-SIN-cerity

We're all, in some way, insincere.
Perhaps you'll recognise yourself here?
The child who says, "I've washed my face,"
The bully who states, "You're in my place!"

The one who says a bad meal is fine,
The woman who claims she's thirty-nine,
The adolescent's drinking brag,
The smile on the front of a glossy mag.

A poker player's daring bluff,
The magician fiddling with his cuff,
The man giving police a made-up name,
That extra-long insurance claim.

The husband replying, "Yes, you're thin!"
The driver who's only had one gin,
Those who say, "The cheque's in the post,"
The one who compliments the most.

The one who laughs at the boss's jokes,
The one who says, "Sincerely, folks!"
You've read this poem and you're not in it?
I don't believe that for one minute!

Leaving Home

A boy from Torbay
To his parents did say,
"Life is a terrible bore,
So I'm going away
To the US of A;
It's time for me to explore.
I'll be able to pay
My way to LA
And spend most of my time on the shore.
So I'm going today,
Don't beg me to stay:
I can't remain home any more.
You'll be sad and go grey,
But it's better this way;
I should have done this before."
His dad said, "Okay,
But make sure, on the way,
You remember to close the door."

Making the Grade

Once I studied oceans
But all my grades were seas.
Then I studied honey
And all my grades were bees.
So I studied dried-up grasses
For many, many days
And was finally rewarded -
Now my grades are 'ays!

Millennium

1000
A thousand years ago,
Vikings came each day
They robbed, destroyed and killed
But apart from that were okay.

1066
Then came the Normans from France,
Which was quite a tiring swim.
Poor old Harold got killed -
An 'arrowing time for him!

1086
Then the Domesday survey;
What a long time it took.
It soon became a best-seller;
Well it was the only book!

1100s
The knights went on crusades
To claim the Holy Land.
I don't know why they bothered -
It was just a load of sand!

1215
King John's Magna Carta;
The barons made him sign.
He promised to be a good ruler,
So they used him to draw a straight line!

1271
Marco Polo set off
On his Chinese expedition.
He was away for many years,
But returned in mint condition!

1314	In the Battle of Bannockburn,
	Robert Bruce managed to win.
	He was inspired by a spider -
	Clearly a master of spin!

1349	Then the Black Death reached England -
	Oh the suffering and the smell.
	A third of Europe perished,
	So the undertakers did well.

1415	The longbowmen of England
	Beat the French at Agincourt.
	They must all have been quite tired;
	Well it was the Hundred Years' War!

1476	Caxton's printing press
	Was developed amidst much hype.
	In Germany there was Gutenberg,
	But we didn't like his type!

1483	Young Edward V and Richard
	Were locked up in the Tower
	During the War of the Roses,
	But why fight over a flower?

1492	Columbus thought he'd found India,
	When he sailed off to the west.
	In fact it was the Caribbean,
	So he failed his geography test!

c.1500

In the sciences and the arts,
Da Vinci was quite a geezer,
But why didn't he put eyebrows
On the face of the Mona Lisa?

1509-47

Henry VIII was a character
Six wives did he take.
Hence the man's obesity -
He just loves wedding cake!

1540s

We're the centre of the universe;
Well that's what folk were taught.
We orbit the Sun, said Copernicus -
A REVOLUTIONary thought!

c.1550

When it came to predicting the future,
Nostradamus was first class.
But he never foresaw Lottery numbers -
A prophet, not profit, alas.

1588

When Philip of Spain attacked,
Drake knew what to do.
"You think you're hard," said Francis,
"But in fact Armada than you!"

c.1600

Then there was Bill Shakespeare,
The brilliant Bard of Avon.
He wrote terrific plays -
In total, thirty-saven!

1605	We should acknowledge Guy Fawkes;
	Never mind the treason and plot,
	Because, for the firework industry,
	He did such an awful lot!
1649	Civil War loser Charles
	Was grabbed by Cromwell's soldiers,
	And made to face the chop,
	Which was quite a weight off his shoulders!
1665	Newton discovered gravity
	When an apple fell on his head.
	He also discovered headaches,
	But of this, little is said.
1665-7	In the same year was The Plague,
	In '66, The Fire was roaring.
	Compared to all this excitement,
	'67 was quite boring!
1733	John Kay's flying shuttle
	Triggered industrialisation;
	Quite a lengthy word to give
	A pretty illiterate nation!
1745	The Jacobite Rebellion failed
	And Bonnie Prince Charlie fled.
	Everyone knew he was male,
	So he dressed as a woman instead!

1773	The colonists in North America
	Paid taxes but had no say,
	So they had their Boston Tea Party
	And the Brits had a taxing day!

c.1780	Who was that eSTEAMed inventor?
	That engineer...that Scot?
	You know him...Watt's-is-name?
	Oh yes, of course, James Watt!

1789-92	Louis XVI craved more power,
	But he started to lose it instead.
	Then he lost his freedom,
	And finally, his head.

1800	Alessandro Volta's battery
	Produced some curious stares.
	It sparked off quite a reaction
	But that's enough of current affairs.

c.1800	Beethoven was the rose
	In the classical music garden.
	"You're a genius!" people would cry,
	And he would answer, "Pardon?"

1805	Nelson won at Trafalgar
	With a plan that you wouldn't believe,
	But as he'd lost his right arm,
	There was room for a trick up his sleeve!

1815	Wellington beat Napoleon
	In the Battle of Waterloo,
	But why at a busy station?
	Why couldn't a big field do?

1815
Wellington beat Napoleon
In the Battle of Waterloo,
But why at a busy station?
Why couldn't a big field do?

1822
Frenchman Joseph Niepce
Started photographing.
It must have been a sad invention,
Because you never saw anyone laughing.

1825
Stephenson's rocket was the first
Steam railway passenger train.
He was helped by his son Robert,
Whom George was able to train!

1851
The Victorian British Empire
Matched that of ancient Rome,
So they built the Crystal Palace -
A sort of glassy Millennium Dome.

1854-6
For the injured and sick in Crimea,
Conditions were so very poor.
Then along came Florence Nightingale,
Who made it a much nicer war.

1859
Darwin's 'Origin of Species'
Really made me think -
Could my hairy, long-armed granny
Be the missing link?

1876	Bell invented the telephone,
	Giving everyone a thrill.
	They were all so very grateful,
	Until they got the bill!

c.1890	Van Gogh was a marvellous artist,
	Painting many masterpieces a year.
	But he always refused a drink,
	Saying, "No thanks, I've got one 'ear!"

1903	People had tried for years
	To master powered flight.
	In the end it was Orville and Wilbur
	Who PLANEly got it Wright!

1908	Ford mass-produced his cars
	To help us get there and back.
	It came in any colour,
	As long as it was black!

1914	Chaplin made his first film;
	Apparently he was funny.
	Odd that being a tramp
	Should bring in so much money.

1914-8	Fourteen million died
	In a sea of mud.
	'The Great War' it was called,
	But it wasn't all that good.

1915	Einstein – what a scientist!
	The finest in the land.
	I'd gladly explain his theories
	But you wouldn't understand.

1926	John Logie Baird's TV
	Has spread much learning and fun,
	But if he's up there watching reality shows,
	He must think, "What have I done?"

1928	Alex Fleming's social life
	Must have been a bit dead,
	To find such fascination
	In a piece of mouldy bread!

1933-45	Hitler thought that everyone
	Should be blue-eyed, blond and tall.
	This was strange because Adolf
	Was dark and rather small.

1939-45	Churchill's leadership helped us
	Through a World War hell.
	He was full of the bulldog spirit,
	And other spirits as well.

1945	America dropped two atom bombs
	Upon the Japanese;
	A slightly heavy-handed way
	To bring them to their knees.

1953   Hillary and Sherpa Tensing
Were the first to Everest's crown.
As Edmund surveyed the scene,
He said, "Cripes, it's a long way down!"

1955   People were quite shocked
By the rock 'n roll of Elvis.
When he first appeared on telly,
They refused to show his pelvis!

1963   JFK was shot,
By Lee Oswald, we thought,
But each year brings a new theory,
So that more books can be bought.

1966   After triumphing over the Germans,
In the First and Second World War,
We beat them once again -
4-2 was the score.

1969   Armstrong was first on the moon,
Buzz Aldrin was the next.
Collins stayed in orbit,
Feeling rather vexed.

1975...   Bill Gates worked with computers
And knew their real worth.
He saw Windows of opportunity
To become the richest man on Earth.

1985	Live Aid brought famine relief,
	For which millions had been praying.
	Further relief was felt
	When some of the bands stopped playing.

1990s	Isn't technology wonderful?
	The internet, mobile phones...
	And if you like somebody,
	You can make genetic clones!

1991	The Soviet Union collapsed;
	For some it was hard to swallow.
	Latvia declared independence
	And others were Russian to follow.

1997	The Americans landed a robot
	Upon the surface of Mars,
	But despite much exploration,
	It found no chocolate bars.

1997	In a Parisian tunnel, Diana,
	Tragically drew her last breath.
	Conspiracy theories abounded -
	For some, a convenient death?

Dec 31, 1999	So it's a special Auld Lang Syne,
	With laughter and with tears.
	Now brace yourself, humanity,
	For the next one thousand years!

MP or MT?

At this point in time,
It is becoming abundantly clear
That in the not too distant future,
Things may be coming to a head.
Isn't it time we stopped beating about the bush?
Isn't it time we laid our cards squarely on the table?
Isn't it time we put an end
To the namby-pamby shilly-shallying?
I believe in facing the music
And shooting straight from the hip.
Let's get down to the nitty-gritty brass tacks
And tackle the problem at grass-roots level
By nipping it in the bud.
The need is being increasingly felt
For us to pull ourselves together,
Put our noses to the grindstone,
Our shoulder to the wheel,
Pull our socks up, roll our sleeves up,
Point our feet in the right direction
And put our best foot forward.
And in the fullness of time,
We can, beyond any shadow of doubt,
Rise to the occasion and hold our own,
But only if we take the rough with the smooth,
Face up to the difficulties ahead
And take the bull by the horns.
But I am not talking about a small bull here.
I am talking a lot of bull.

My First Romance

Butterflies in my stomach,
Ants are in my pants.
I've got insects everywhere;
This is my first romance.
Someone said she likes me
But I didn't get too excited;
She only finds me handsome
'Cos she's a bit short-sighted.
So we're going out tonight
But I've no idea where,
And I couldn't find my mousse,
So I couldn't do my hair!
To give me fresh-breath confidence,
I had to buy some mints,
'Cos last time I was near her,
I'm sure I saw her wince.
I won't know what to talk about;
I don't think she likes sport.
She likes to do embroidery
But I'm not the sewing sort.
Well now the time has come;
I walk to Mandy's house.
My heart is thumping madly,
I'm as timid as a mouse.
It's Mandy's mum who answers
And to my disbelief,
She says that Mandy's poorly.
Phew, what a relief!

My Dad

(I read this poem out at my dad's 65th birthday party in 1992.)

Welcome friends and relations
To these celebrations
In honour of Norman, my dad.
Though he's reached humpty-five,
He continues to thrive
And his table tennis isn't too bad.

Comedian, singer,
Happiness bringer,
A student of world history,
Kibbutznik, librarian,
Humanitarian -
Yes they're all things he'd like to be!

This man has brought pleasure
In no meagre measure
To thousands of people I'm sure.
With his brand of hilarity,
He's helped many a charity,
Though they've heard all his jokes before!

Now dad's playing Tevye,
A little older and heavier
Than when he played him in seventy four,
But I have no doubt
That talent will out
And he'll over-shlog* Topol once more.

(* Yiddish for outdo)

Now my thirst for knowledge
Came from him, not from college;
When it comes to wisdom, he's top.
I'd drive him so mad,
Saying, "Ask me things, dad!"
And he would – he'd ask me to stop!

Whenever he can,
He spends time with our Dan
And they've struck up this marvellous rapport.
He's made Daniel dotty
About Pavarotti.
Now it's 'Nessun Dorma' encore!

Tonight, please don't mention
Bob Maxwell's pension -
It caused a slight commotion.
At last dad's been paid;
How much has he made?
You could say it's a drop in the ocean!

Behind each great man
Is a good woman,
And of course there's one behind dad.
She's strong and she's witty,
Devoted and pretty,
But if mum finds out, she'll go mad!

So it fills me with pride
To have this man by my side -
So humorous, gentle and warm.
Now our thoughts we must quench,
As we drink to this mensch* –
To life, lechayim^, to Norm!

(* Yiddish - a decent person, ^ a Hebrew toast meaning 'to life!')

A Mystery Lesson

Life is a mystery, don't you agree?
Like why is the evening meal called tea?
Where do socks hide in the washing machine?
Why is milk white if grass is green?

Why don't cuckoos build a nest?
What happened to the crew of the Marie Celeste?
Why should a black cat bring you luck?
Why is there a fish called a Bombay duck?

Why do you stand for a seat as MP?
And why do you sit in the stands at Wembley?
In the Arctic, how do creatures survive?
Is Elvis Presley still alive?

Why boxing 'ring' when it's a square?
Why don't women lose their hair?
Why do actors say 'break a leg'?
Which DID come first – chicken or egg?

Where is the beginning of the sky?
What happens to us when we die?
If you have answers to these queries,
Please write to me with your theories.

Naughty Norman

Naughty Norman gets no thanks
For getting up to silly pranks.
He drops things upon your head,
Puts plastic spiders in your bed.
He disrupts class with a silly cough,
He rings your doorbell, then runs off.
He will put, given half a chance,
Itching powder in your pants!
He takes sweets from smaller boys,
When you're asleep, he makes a noise.
He loosens the top of the pepper pot,
So instead of a bit, you get a lot!
He puts some powder in your drink,
So when you wee, it comes out pink!
One of Norman's very worst sins
Is carefully-placed banana skins,
And watch out for his special treat -
Black shoe polish on the toilet seat!
Now that I've told you, don't do the same,
'Cos if you do, I'll get the blame!

Ode to an Ex-Gillfriend

There are plenty of other fish in the sea,
But you were but my bream girl.
We had a whale of a time.
Do you remember that plaice we went to,
Where it cost ten squid to get in?
But I'm not going to carp.
Then I took you to see the Halle, but
You said you preferred sole music.
We spent the Oyster holidays together;
All we did was skate and play crabbage.
Then suddenly you decided to clam up.
You started annoying me on porpoise.
I knew there was salmon else;
He was Ray, the plastic sturgeon.
How could you fall for that little shrimp?
He's got no mussels
And wears a herring-aid.
I suppose I haddock coming to me -
The whiting was on the wall.
Perhaps I was a little shell-fish;
Cod knows, I tried not to be.
Now I am left to mullet over.
I think of those happy dace we spent.
My heart will never 'eel.
You left such a haking gap in my life.
There will never be anyone to fillet.

Oh Brother!

I used to drink, oh brothers,
All day and through the night,
But that is all behind me,
And now I'm (hic) alright!

Oh how I used to gamble,
But brothers, now I'm through,
And if you don't believe me,
A fiver says it's true!

Brothers, I once swore a lot,
Cursed with all my might,
But now I have been cured,
I've seen the b*****n' light!

Brothers how I used to fight,
But I'm rescued from that sin.
Should any of you doubt it,
I'll smash your face right in!

I used to be untruthful.
I still am, you realise,
So this whole story, brothers,
Is just a pack of lies!

O Limp Ian!

I know a young man called Ian,
Who's lazy, lethargic and limp.
He never makes much of an effort -
In fact he's a bit of a wimp.
Partaking in sporting endeavours
Has always been something to hate,
Yet he can put in a claim
To be an Olympic great!
'Cos he's good at throwing tantrums,
His nose runs quite a bit,
And he tends to jump to conclusions,
So he's clearly keeping fit!
He wrestles with his conscience,
Hurls insults at the cat,
Runs into trouble generally,
No wonder he's not fat!
He does the crawl each morning -
That's traffic-crawl to town,
And rows with all his neighbours
(That works better written down!)
He skips responsibilities,
Can really catch a cold,
But though he's such an athlete,
He's got no chance of a gold!

Once Bittern, Twice Shy

Oh, Henrietta!
You were my special gullfriend,
Migrate love.
We had such fun larking around.
I tweeted you so well.
I had a nest-egg put aside -
Admittedly a poultry sum -
For our eaglely awaited marriage.
But then things took a tern for the worse.
That was when you met Robin,
The petrel-pump attendant
From Finchley.
He was a swift worker;
He took you off to the Canary Islands.
That was hard to swallow.
I still thought eider chance,
But then there was Jack Daw
and Albert Ross.
You even began to crow about it.
You became so unpheasant
And displayed such a fowl temper.
Well now I'm glad it's owl over.
I have no egrets.
You're so cheep.
I'm off to the Falcon Islands.
Don't eggspeck me back.

Over the Limit

Oh Sherry! She was such a bubbly girl!
I was hoping we'd have some tots together
But now our days of wine and roses
Have come to a bitter end.
Guess she just grew Bordeaux me.
Maybe I was too mild-mannered.
I let her go out with ouzoever she wanted.
I knew there was trouble brewing,
When she met Sam Buca,
An arrogant, saki character,
Who dressed so Chablis.
How could you beer-tracted to him?
I was sangria than I'd ever been before -
Really wanted to give them both a punch.
Yet I still thought perhap cider chance.
Maybe we could be-gin again?
Thought absinthe might make her heart fonder?
But now it seems she has no rum for me in her life.
Vodkan I do about it?
I've given up all hop.
I'm so dispirited.
But it's time to stop wining.
Now I just want tequila.
One shot should do it.

Planet Geoff

Scientists have found a planet
Called Kepler 186f.
It's not a very catchy name;
I think I'll call it Geoff.

What makes it rather interesting
Is that it resembles Earth.
I don't wish to be sizeist
But it's of slightly greater girth.

It's in the 'Goldilocks' zone -
Not too hot, not too cold -
But there's no porridge on Geoff;
At least that's what I'm told.

It's 500 light years away;
So wormhole travel would do,
But I'd still take extra sandwiches
And more paper for the loo.

I think I would travel to Geoff;
It's a bit of a gamble I know.
I might not get Sky Sports there
And the chance of a romance is low.

But it's got to be better than Earth
With its wars and crime and disease,
So I'd better start saving up now -
A one-way ticket please!

A Poem for the Nineties

BSE
CJD
HIV
Tablets of 'E'
Global warming
Ozone holes forming
Mobile phones
Genetic clones
Road rage
The litigious age
Mandela is freed
Viagra – if you need!
The National Lottery
Virtual reality
The Teletubbies
New Age hubbies
Ofsted reports
Drugs in sports
Get a cyberpet!
Get on the internet!
School league tables
TV by cables
Joyriders in cars
Robots on Mars
Have your cholesterol checked
Be politically correct

Turn European!
Cruise the Caribbean!
Zero tolerance
Designer underpants
The end of apartheid
Rwandan genocide
Football's coming home
The Millennium Dome
Spice Girls everywhere
Man United silverware
The Bosnian crisis
Legalise cannabis
Labour back in
Doctors of spin
Things paranormal
Royals less formal
A chauffeur's madness
A nation's sadness
What a cornucopia
Not quite Utopia

A Pupil's Lament

I don't like school;
It's not very cool,
All that learning and stuff.
I can write and read -
What more do I need?
I already know quite enough.

I can't see the attraction
In dividing a fraction,
Or working in different bases.
And please don't mention
Comprehension -
I just leave lots of spaces.

Some say it's a blast
To study the past,
But why bother about times that have gone?
A science experiment
Would add to my merriment,
But the teacher just goes on and on.

And I'm supposed to learn
About each country in turn,
But they're so far away, who cares?
And assembly's so boring,
I just feel like snoring -
I don't see the point of those prayers.

In music, the theory

Is so very dreary,

That I sing in the silliest way.

I like to do art,

But by the time that we start,

It's time to put stuff away.

Every summer I cram

For some stupid exam,

Though the facts are soon forgotten.

And as for the food,

By the time that I've queued,

The choice that's left is rotten.

PE should be fun,

But we roll, jump and run,

As if we're performing seals.

All in all, education?

I prefer the vacation -

Now THAT part of school still appeals!

Postman Pat-hetic

At number one,
A dog tries it on,
And takes a chunk out of my calf.
At number two,
A card won't go through,
So I have to tear it in half.
At number three,
I bang my knee
Trying to jump a wall.
And at number four,
They've got no front door,
So I just drop their mail in the hall.
I hate number five,
With its very long drive,
So I deliver just once a week.
And at number six,
There's a boy who throws sticks,
So I give his nose a tweak.
At number seven,
There's a nutter called Kevin;
The less said of him, the better.
At number eight,
I can't open the gate,
So they never receive a letter!
At number nine,
There's some little swine
Who rides his bike over my feet.
And at number ten,
My bag splits again;
All the letters are blown down the street!

Second Degree Murder

Having gone to university,
To obtain a pretty good degree,
My wife is doing an MSc;
An admirable thing, you will agree.
She's studying conscientiously,
Reading books assiduously,
Taking notes most copiously,
But she doesn't manage easily.
She has a job as well, you see,
And several kids, including me!
We all suffer accordingly,
As she is very rarely free.
There are times, nocturnally,
When I'd like a cuddle, naturally;
I may nudge her affectionately,
But she must finish chapter three.
And so I enter celibacy,
Not a little reluctantly.
Instead I choose to watch TV,
But that's forbidden, frustratingly -
It's too distracting, apparently.
And so it goes, interminably.
At times I feel, understandably,
Like committing murder, second degree!

A Shining Example

I've always stated
That hair's overrated;
So much fuss and expense.
Think of all you must do,
With comb and shampoo,
So be bald – you know it makes sense.

Yes, lose all your hair
And you won't have a care;
The embarrassment is but tiny.
Your hair? Just abolish it.
Your head? You just polish it!
It looks really good when it's shiny!

So come one and all,
Be a billiard ball!
It's time for eggheads to rejoice.
But one thing I must state,
About my bald pate,
Is that sadly I haven't a choice!

Sick of Waiting

I hate going to the doctor's
It gets right on my wick;
All those coughing, sneezing whingers -
They really make me sick!
There's nothing wrong with any of them;
It's obvious I'm the worst.
I hurt my little finger,
So I should be the first,
But instead I have to wait
And read a women's magazine
That's been lying around the surgery
Since nineteen seventeen.
I decided to read the notices
Stuck up on the wall,
But I've not got flu or asthma,
So they're no use at all.
Eventually my name is called;
I approach the doctor's door,
But I've had to wait so very long,
My finger hurts no more!

Sofa, So Good

I looked down the back of the sofa,
Hoping to find my pen,
But instead I found a penny,
So I thought I'd try again.
I thrust my hand down the back
And found a half-eaten sweet.
It was sticky and somewhat fluffy,
So I gave it to dad as a treat.
Encouraged by my findings,
I had another look
And I came across the last page
Of an Agatha Christie book!
I tried the side next time
And discovered several holes:
In one I found a comb
And three remote controls!
This is fun, I thought,
As I reached down really far,
And solved the lengthy mystery
Of our missing budgerigar!
There's probably nothing left now
But I think I'll try once more.
There's something large and furry;
What is it? Oh – the floor!

So Shallow Me Dear!

Whilst social media sites are great

To inform, amuse, communicate,

I click Facebook with some trepidation -

Who will be my next irritation?

Some people only want to post

Whenever they get the urge to boast.

And yes I know your kids are nice

But just ONE picture will suffice.

Don't ask me to play Candy Crush Saga -

Ask me to the pub for a pint of lager.

And why must you check in everywhere you go?

"I'm now on the loo" - we don't need to know.

And do you think we're filled with glee,

To hear, once more, you're at Terminal 3?

Or when it's fairly wet or cold,

Do we really need to be told?

"I'm so tired!" - well hold the front page!

My irritation turns to rage.

You know that symbol with the upturned thumb?

I think we need one for 'talking through bum'.

You're just a social media friend.

You're just so shallow me dear. The end.

Technophobe

I'm having a bit of trouble
With technological terms,
For example I thought a virus
Was all about bad germs.
I thought that RAM and mouse
Were creatures – silly me,
And I thought that someone's laptop
Was their leg, above their knee.
I considered chips and cookies
To be just a tasty snack,
And I thought that someone's hard disc
Explained their aching back.
I understood that 'website'
Meant what a spider could see,
And when you said megahertz,
That you were in agony.
Now everyone's got a tablet
But apparently that's not a pill,
And I thought 'high definition'
Was a dictionary on a hill!
I thought when you said 'browser'
It meant that you weren't buying,
And when you were online
Your clothes were hung up, drying.

'Information superhighway' -
Is it the traffic report today?
And I was convinced that Jpeg
Was between pegs I and K!
I thought when you entered a chat room,
You'd just gone down the pub,
And when you talked of megabytes,
You'd eaten lots of grub.
I thought the phrase 'cloud storage'
Was another term for rain,
And when you said 'search engine',
It meant you'd lost your train.
When you bought a flash drive,
I thought you meant sports car,
And when you mentioned multiplex,
You meant the cinemar!
I thought digital compression
Was when someone trod on your shoe,
And that when you had downloaded,
You'd just been for a poo!
So I am technophobic,
As you can clearly see,
And although my son's an expert,
I'm afraid IT's lost on me!

Time Flies

I made a rocket the other night,
Which, surprisingly, went faster than light.
I found myself able to travel through time;
I saw me, with hair, in my prime.
There was me, as a young man,
Trying to teach, trying to plan.
Then I was cringing – my toes did curl,
As I saw teenage me try to chat up a girl.
I watched, in horror, myself, aged ten,
Fighting with siblings, again and again.
I witnessed myself as a three-year-old boy
Breaking some other child's toy!
I went back to a time before I was born,
But the elastic band was getting quite worn.
I reached the year my mum was thirteen
But crash-landed on her in my machine.
She didn't survive – I wish I'd missed,
Because as a result, I no longer exist!

Training

Carrying my heavy case through a crowded town;
Why is all the way uphill – why can't it be down?
And with this bloomin' rainstorm, if I don't collapse, I'll drown,
But I've not got the strength to even frown.

People keep on jostling me, as through the town they race,
Especially old ladies with the minimum of grace,
So I try to knock them over with my big brown case,
But they just wave umbrellas in my face.

I stagger bravely onwards, my clothes are wringing wet,
Partly from the driving rain, partly from the sweat.
I hurry to the station, for I've a train to get,
But I'm too slow and getting quite upset.

Surely it's not possible a case can put on weight?
If only it had wheels, I would not be in this state.
My heart is thumping madly at a quite alarming rate,
But a hernia will surely be my fate.

I crawl into the station with great relief and glee;
Soon I can put my case down – my limbs will soon be free.
I make it to the platform, where someone says to me,
"It's just gone out – the next is half past three!"

Triskaidekaphobia*

Since I moved house to number thirteen,
I've had bad luck with every machine.
The microwave went on the blink
And the waste disposal just blocks the sink.
The washing machine makes everything dirty
And the kitchen clock says twenty-five thirty.
The telly has pictures but alas, no sound
And the hoover just moves the dirt around.
The lawnmower likes to attack the bushes
And the downstairs loo no longer flushes.
The oven burns the kitchen foil
And the kettle takes two days to boil.
The telephone rings when no-one calls
And the food processor decorates the walls.
The DVD player will not rewind
And my camera seems to have gone quite blind.
The dishwasher is completely shot
And the fridge just makes everything hot.
So the sensible thing, it seems to me,
Is to change my address to number 12b!

(* A fear of number thirteen)

Undergrad Engineers

(This was written in 1975 when I was a student at Bradford University. Students on engineering courses seemed to acquire a certain reputation – most unfairly of course.)

Too much denim and not enough silk.
Too much booze and not enough milk.
Too much fun and too few worries.
Too few greens and too many curries.
Too little poetry, too much swearing.
Too much crudity, too little caring.
Too few leaders and too many sheep.
Too many late nights, not enough sleep.
Too many lads and not enough lasses.
Too many re-sits, not enough passes.
Too much spending, not enough saving.
Too little quietude, too much raving.
Too few listen, too few work.
Too many shout, too many shirk.
Too many insults, too many sneers,
Too many bloody engineers!

Unlucky

I bought some vinegar but it went off.
I saw Pavarotti but he had a cough.
My toast always lands buttered side down.
I once had a goldfish which managed to drown.
I'd scored ninety-nine then I hit my wicket.
I thought I'd won a raffle but I'd lost my ticket.
All my photos come out blurred.
I often get bombed by a passing bird.
In football, I usually hit the post.
It always rains when I go to the coast.
All my shoes either pinch or rub.
Every apple I eat contains a grub.
My dog always howls whenever I'm singing.
My neighbour's alarm is always ringing.
When I yawn in the summer, I swallow a fly.
I once missed a UFO go by.
I love curry but I'm allergic to rice.
And I've been struck by lightning – twice!
But I am quite lucky in one respect:
I can write poems that rhyme perfect-
ly.
Oops!

When the Coach Stopped

When the coach stopped,
The botanist got out to go behind a bush.
The politician got out to bring something up.
The juggler got out to throw up.
The hypochondriac got out to be sick.
The snooker player got out for a rest.
The India rubber man got out to stretch his legs.
The bald man got out for a bit of fresh 'air.
The Yorkshireman got owt for nowt.
The Scotsman got out for a wee moment.
The cricketer got out for a duck.
The duck got out for a lark.
The chicken got out to fowl the footpath.
The horse got out for a bit.
The chameleon got out for a change.
The philosopher got out for a reason
And the poet got out
Because he couldn't think of a good ending.

What a State We're In!

America's invaded the world;
No, not in a military sense.
I mean their culture is everywhere
And it makes me quite incensed.

If you go to any country
And enter any house,
I bet the people living there
Have heard of Mickey Mouse.

Now I've seen many people
From Maoris up to Lapps,
But instead of national costumes,
They all wear baseball caps!

You'll see t-shirts, jeans and trainers
In Lima and in Laos,
And guess who's on their t-shirts?
You guessed it – Mickey Mouse!

I've been to Kuala Lumpur,
Kiev and Katmandu;
They've all seen Spiderman movies
And probably Batman too.

MacNuggets, MacMuffins, MacChicken –
It really makes me ill.
Will it soon be MacBread and MacWater?
Will whales be eating MacKrill?

And once, in the Amazon Jungle,
A pygmy got in my way.
I thought he was going to eat me,
But he just said, "Have a nice day!"

On the Great Wall of China,
Built thousands of years ago,
Some American tourist
Had simply written, "Yo!"

Millions of little children,
From the Nile to the Mekong,
Instead of traditional music,
Sing a Michael Jackson song!

You may think what does it matter?
It's not exactly a sin.
But we're losing our rich cultures;
What a (fifty-first) state we're in!

Win or Blues

No-one is perfect,
We've all got a defect;
Perhaps you're a terrible boozer.
In faults I am rich,
The biggest of which,
Is that I'm a terrible loser.

You see, I've never reckoned
On finishing second;
I've always got to be first.
So my mental condition
Rests on my position,
Which is usually one of the worst.

When I am defeated,
I feel I've been cheated;
My opponent was clearly sinning.
I can't explain t'ya -
Perhaps megalomania -
But I've got this mad passion for winning.

So if I don't do well,
I'll make your life hell;
I'll fume and I'll foam and I'll fret.
But I find it confusing,
That I can't stand losing,
With all the practice I get!

The Worst Tattooist

I am the worst tattooist,
So I wouldn't come to me.
I once etched 'Leeds Untied'
On some unfortunate's knee.

One girl wanted 'Arsenal'
On her lower back, in pink,
But after just four letters,
I ran right right out of ink!

A lovesick man came in -
I never meant him harm -
But I carved 'I vole Sarah'
Into his upper arm.

A woman wanted a flower
Upon a bottom cheek.
It should have taken an hour,
But I made it last all week!

My shop's called 'Pains and Needles';
If you see me, don't come in,
For you will lose your money,
Plus lots of blood and skin!

You

You're the fly in the ointment,
You're the nail in a tyre,
You're the metal in a microwave,
You're the flat voice in a choir.

You're the crumbs in a bed,
You're the crack in a jug,
You're the worm in an apple,
You're the salt on a slug.

You're the shell in an omelette,
You're the spoiler of jokes,
You're the Lego under bare feet,
You're the stick in the spokes.

You're the rain during cricket,
You're the stone in a shoe,
You're the pork at a barmitzvah,
You're the blockage in the loo.

Well I think you've got the message,
I could go on like this all day,
But I'd better get on with my life,
And put this mirror away.